Forward (and onward)	
It sort of began in Belgium	
Back to the present	5
Ensure your seat is	6
in the upright position	6
'Customs'. It's kind of	7
a clue in the title	7
Names have been withheld,	9
to protect the living	9
The Really Useful Bits	10
Motorway Patrol	12
Are you feeling hungry?	14
'The Wrong Island'	18
Absolutely, positively Wellington	19
Little baches, little baches	22
A whale of a time?	24
Trust me, that's not a tail	26
'Glowworm' sounds prettier	28
Hebe heaven	29
The Shaky Isles	31
Hubble, bubble…	34
Top to toe	35
And finally…	36

**AUCKLAND FROM THE WATER, WITH THE SKY TOWER.
THE COVER PICTURE IS WELLINGTON AIRPORT, FROM MOUNT VICTORIA**

Forward (and onward)

This little book is an affectionate look at a wonderful country that will hopefully be of use and interest to anyone contemplating spending many hours in a metal tube at 30,000 feet to get there.

It is a 'work in progress' because I hope to get back there some day. And because with active volcanoes and earthquakes – like Kaikoura's in 2016, which raised parts of the seabed – New Zealand itself isn't set in stone.

Cassie Graham lives in a lumpy part of the UK, with a neurotic, OCD dog and some freeloading wood mice.

SUNRISE IN PAIHIA

It sort of began in Belgium

A little about the author (that's me)

His name was Chris. (Still is, I guess).

I was a day past my 20th birthday, he was a not-long-qualified doctor and we first got talking in Belgium.

We partnered each other, against two fellow travellers, at cards through to Germany. I let him kiss me in Copenhagen and The Beatles' song 'Norwegian Wood' has always had a certain meaning for me since.

It came to an end in Amsterdam when he pushed me into a canal – well, shallow culvert thing.

But somewhere along the way, he'd taken a tourist leaflet map of northern Europe and inked in, upside down, two islands to show the place he called home.

He lasted for that one summer trip. The interest he sparked in me in New Zealand was to last a lot, lot longer.

That would be a good point to fast forward to when I finally made it to his home city of Christchurch. But it's not the whole story.

Instead, let me take you just a year later, to a never-to-be-forgotten night in Florence.

It had rained all day, and the friend I was travelling with and I had traipsed round endless marble monuments and decided to knock back some duty free vodka, with orange, back at the campsite to 'thaw out' before going out for the evening.

There was a meal in a restaurant where the wine flowed free as long as you were eating. So the incentive was there to drink it quickly (and eat slowly!) and get it replenished.

And then there were the zombies.

Not actual undead people. But the name of a cocktail served at the Red Garter nightclub, where entry was conditional on you buying one. And a whole bunch of us were having fun and one cocktail was never going to last all night.

Getting lost on the way back, we asked a prostitute in the end. She kindly pointed us the right way, while her friend talked through the window into a car, to a potential customer.

Back at the campsite, I got a bit confused after the toilet block, when it came to finding where I was going to sleep. To my rescue came Phil.

In Rome, a day or two later, he kindly chucked my washing in the machine with his. Shame he'd put a red sweatshirt in, but I didn't mind all my stuff coming out pink.

I returned the kindness in Munich, by which time, I'd decided his home, Bay of Islands, sounded lovely and well worth a visit.

27 years later, I stepped off a bus in Paihia, Bay of Islands. I had finally made it.

It was raining

THE ORIGINAL MAP!

A GLIMPSE OF FRANZ JOSEF GLACIER, LEFT, AND BELOW

Back to the present

Reading a book I'd bought years ago: a bloke's trip round New Zealand. I'd abandoned it first time because I didn't take to the author much. Still don't, but I could read it now to compare his experiences to mine. Because in the meantime, I'd visited pretty much all the places in his book.

He wrote it with a flat tone of gloom I reckon would put a lot of prospective tourists off who didn't know any better.

And I thought: "I could write the same book myself, only I'd be a lot more positive."

I may be a 'late developer' when it comes to venturing to the southern hemisphere – career and family took over my life, delaying the realisation of my 'dream'. But I've been round the world five times in five years, explored the Shaky Isles from northern tip to southern toe. And not only have I got under the skin of New Zealand, but it has got under mine.

If that's not making you itch uncomfortably, read on.

AUCKLAND AIRPORT AT SUNRISE

Ensure your seat is in the upright position

Happy landings

My first glimpse of Aotearoa, the land of the long white cloud, was exciting, but not in the good way I'd been anticipating.

It came after a week's stop-over in Hong Kong. A week, in my humble view, being plenty, as it's very much a working city/administrative region and not very tourist-y. Unless you have a mind to buy "copy watches," "copy handbags," or even "genuine copy handbags" from annoying men in suits accosting you every few yards. Or wish to have your fortune told by someone who claims to have once lived in West Ham.

(He was shooed away by a policeman, whose arrival I considered good fortune indeed).

Anyway, seat belts were fastened, seat-back trays folded up, and the plane was straining and clanking and making all the horrible noises they do when trying to get from 32,000 feet to ground level through assorted layers of cloud and pressure.

Looking out of the window, we seemed to be skimming waves, with no sign of actual land at all.

And just as I was assuring myself the pilot and co-pilot wouldn't be doing this if all there was ahead of them was ocean, the plane clonked down very lopsidedly on to something solid, before the other side flopped down to join it on terra firma.

I was tired, long-haul-flight weary, and my heart was returning from my mouth. But I was also thrilled because while it had taken me 27 years to get there, I was finally in New Zealand.

HOBBITON

'Customs'. It's kind of a clue in the title

On arrival

Very few NZ television programmes find their way on to the airwaves in the UK. One that does is Passport Patrol: a reality show about the work of customs, the Ministry of Agriculture and Forestry, the immigration service, etc.

It quite often features irate or tearful arrivals at airports, upset at being given grief and informing the official and the TV crew they don't think much of the welcome and will never visit New Zealand again.

The officials never, ever give in to the temptation to reply: "Bog off, then."

My arrivals have always been trouble-free. I have always felt I was being welcomed.

I'm sure anyone reading this is far too sensible to need the following advice, but here it is anyway.

If you'd like my experience, rather than the other:

- fill in your arrivals card properly before landing
- if you must partake of drugs, don't wear clothes that have had them in the pockets or anything else that will carry traces a sniffer dog can detect
- respect that you are about to be a guest of the country you are visiting, their rules are their rules, and not to be argued with, whatever you think you should be entitled to do.

- get it into your head that "food" means "anything edible".

New Zealand is a stunningly beautiful country, with interesting wildlife, and an economy that is heavily dependent on agriculture.

They do not want this destroyed by some disease or pest 'imported' into the country by someone who thinks he/she is above the biosecurity rules, or someone who doesn't quite get that nuts are food and mud on camping equipment is not sterile.

As a first world country, New Zealand has supermarkets, convenience stores, restaurants, cafés... you will not starve if you fail to smuggle in your favourite snacks from home.

As far as immigration are concerned: you don't need to account for every planned second of your proposed stay. But if you have no accommodation lined up at all, very little money or evidence of access to it, and no idea what you want to see now you've arrived, it may look a little suspicious.

You may be asked if you have a return or onward ticket. "Welcome to New Zealand – when are you leaving?" But it's nothing personal.

Follow the yellow brick road

If Auckland isn't your final destination, once through the control area, you have to amble round from the international terminal to the domestic.

To get there/back, you simply follow the blue and white lines painted on the pavement/road. Or the green line, as it had been repainted by my fourth trip.

It's simple and brilliant. No language issues, and if you've just travelled 11,000 miles straight from the UK and don't what day it is or which way is up, following those lines is probably about as much as your brain will be up to.

Once on your domestic flight, you will be offered coffee/tea, and a choice of a mini packet of cassava chips, biscuits, or 'lollies'.

Congratulations: you have just learned your first NZ word. Lollies are not lollipops, but sweets.

I recommend the chips.

A HELPFUL SIGNPOST AT DRIVING CREEK NARROW GAUGE RAILWAY, ON THE COROMANDEL PENINSULA

LAKE WANAKA, IN THE OTAGO REGION, COVERS 192 KM2 (74 SQ MILES)

Names have been withheld, to protect the living

A word about accommodation

My first visit to NZ lasted five weeks and was spent entirely with a good friend, and with his family. It's one thing to namecheck people no one can identify and another to include people I care about very much who could be recognised.

I have decided to leave out references to them for their privacy, rather than because I don't appreciate their hospitality.

On which topic: you will notice there isn't a chapter headed 'accommodation'. A pretty key thing to leave out? Well yes, but Things Change. At least one hostel I've stayed at and would have recommended has since been closed, because it would have cost too much to bring it up to earthquake-safety standards. Others may still exist but not be as nice as they were, or be nicer. Personally, I've not stayed at an NZ YHA I didn't like and as well as being cheap, hostels are a great place to meet people from around the world. Visit www.yha.co.nz/hostels/ for a current list.

There are hundreds of other nice hostels in places the YHA does and doesn't cover, along with nice hotels, motels, holiday parks, lodges, campsites, B&Bs... or you could rent a motorhome and like a snail, take it with you.

ACTIVE VOLCANO RUAPEHU HAS TWO SKI FIELDS IN WINTER

The Really Useful Bits

A few topics so important, they can have their own section where they won't get lost amid other things.

Slip, slop, slap

First up: wear suntan lotion. The ozone layer above NZ is thin. Twenty minutes' exposure to the sun without suncream and if you have pale skin, you will look like a boiled lobster.

Slap, slap, scratch

Second. Unlike its trans-Tasman neighbour Australia, the wildlife of New Zealand is benign. Nothing is out to kill you. However, certain places have an insect which is evil spawn of hell: the sand fly.

Sandflies are found at beaches, and at the edges of lakes or swamps. Only two species bite, and of those, only the females bite. But boy, is that more than enough.

Captain James Cook was no wuss. But even he took issue with the things, writing in his journal in 1773: 'The most mischievous animal here is the small black sand fly which are exceeding numerous … wherever they light they cause a swelling and such intolerable itching that it is not possible to refrain from scratching and at last ends in ulcers like the small Pox.'

One biting species is found on the North Island, but it's the South where you'll encounter them big time. If you are visiting West Coast and Fiordland, it is wise to bathe regularly in insect repellent.

Drip, drip, drop

Third, the weather. You are visiting New Zealand. You are not visiting Australia: it's more than 2,000km away. That's about the distance from Glasgow to Athens, and you don't expect Glasgow to be hot and sunny all year round. New Zealand has ski slopes in places. It has rainforest. It has the same seasons as the UK, only 'in reverse'. Check the rough forecast for the time you're staying and pack accordingly.

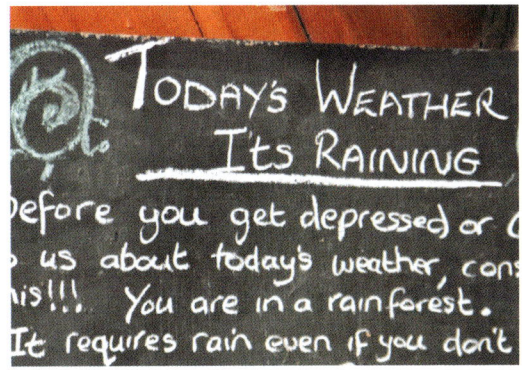

The weather forecast pictured was in a café at Pukékura

Slip, risk a slap

Fourthly, accents. Which can be as thorny as leptospermum (aka manuka, aka the New Zealand tea tree).

This advice applies mostly when you are somewhere else, obviously: when you hear an Antipodean accent in NZ, odds are high the speaker will be a Kiwi.

Australians take the mickey out of the Kiwi accent. Kiwis get very upset at being mistaken for Australians. If you really can't 'till the duffrunce' (that was a clue) between the two, play it safe. Don't act 'clever' and ask: "So what part of Australia are you from?" as you will feel decidedly un-clever if the person replies huffily that they are not. Instead, ask: "So where are you from, then?"

If they just say the country, THEN you can act clever: "Yeah, I meant whereabouts in…"

I use this one when I have no idea if someone is Canadian/American.

Finally, sheep. If you ask innocent and genuine questions of New Zealanders like 'where can we see the kangaroos?' they will try not to laugh at your ignorance. Well, not in front of you. Say the wrong thing about sheep and a man is more likely to look angry than amused, and assume you are taking the p*. Unless you have some overwhelmingly important reason to do so, avoid the topic.

*that's 'proverbial'.

PALMERSTON NORTH BUS STATION

Motorway Patrol

Getting about

As I've already said, few NZ telly shows find their way to UK screens and for a while, if you wanted to hear those lovely vowels it was choice between Passport Patrol and Motorway Patrol.

If you've seen the latter, you may imagine NZ has motorways aplenty.

They don't.

There are stretches at Auckland and a chunk at Wellington that slices through an historic cemetery. 199 kilometres in total.

To put this in perspective, there are 11,000 kilometres of State Highway roads on the two islands, and 83,000 km of local roads (of which only 61 per cent have a tarsealed surface, the rest being chippings).

There are trains. But these are generally referred in disparaging tones. Seventy per cent of freight and 80 per cent of personal travel is by road.

If you want to hire a car, well they drive on the left, as in the UK, but they deal in kilometres, not miles.

Which a kind British couple who gave me a lift once at Waitomo appeared not to have realised, as she stuck rigidly to a speed of 40kph on a (luckily) empty road.

They recently changed the laws on giving way at junctions and a lot of Kiwis had no idea what the changes meant, but that should've settled by now. Possibly after creating a lot of custom for body repair shops.

If you don't want to drive, there are some excellent bus services.

The long-distance ones, you need to book your seat in advance (like National Express). Unlike the UK, the driver will give you a great commentary on the places you're driving through and the rest stops (toilets, cafés) are way nicer than any motorway service station.

If you invest in a travel pass, you may find yourself on a service really designed for young backpackers on a tight budget.

As a less-young backpacker, these can be entertaining or annoying, but that's public transport for you.

One trip was broken up by the (Aussie) driver organising a game of 'bus skittles'. Down the aisle of the coach, using plastic bottles, each passenger having a go, and doing it on the move. Which probably wasn't a great idea from a health and safety point of view. One the one hand, it reminded me of a bus crash I was involved in in Belgium, where the only people hurt (other than minor cuts from flying glass) were the two not wearing seat belts. One the other, it reminded me of Top Deck holidays as a student, cooking meals for everyone else on two gas rings on a double-decker bus as it rattled round Norway. And it was fun.

I was on one Intercity bus that was pulled over by the police, so they could remove some lad they were after, before we were let on our way again.

All part of life's rich tapestry.

It's also a good way to get chatting to new people, or just to eavesdrop them.

On an Intercity bus, as it left Picton ferry terminal heading for Christchurch, I heard an American man ask the driver: "Have you driven to Christchurch before?"

Later, as we enjoyed amazing views of the Pacific Ocean to our left, he inquired: "Do you get fish from there?"

And there was a pleasant, but earnest American on another bus, who told me he was reading a biography of James Cook.

I said: "Don't want to spoil it for you, but it ends very badly".

Then thought perhaps that was a bit off, joking to a stranger.

But he replied that he knew, as he'd visited the spot in Hawaii where Cook was killed.

Nice Conversations I have Enjoyed on Buses would take a chapter in itself.

It really is a great way to share a while with nice people you will never see again.

When on foot, a quick heads-up on crossing the roads. Pelican (light-controlled) crossings aren't the same as in the UK. And not just the distinctive 'beep, beep, beep' which is different from our 'beep, beep, beep' and a sound that always makes me smile, when I first arrive, as a reminder I HAVE arrived.

The difference is that whereas in the UK, a green light for pedestrians mean the traffic is stopped in all directions, in NZ, vehicles can still turn into the road you are crossing – they just have to give to way to you.

Also, the 'green man' stays green for a very short time. Vehicles aren't allowed to run you over if you've started to cross the road, so you don't have to be a 100m sprinter to get across in that time.

AN OLD SIGN IN WELLINGTON

Are you feeling hungry?

Some local specialities

Did you try to bring all your favourite foods with you, only to have them confiscated at the airport, along with a $400 fine? Of course not, you're far too sensible.

Food and drink in NZ are by and large the same as in the UK. With a few tweaks.

If you like sweet potato, the supermarket shelves have a great choice of different colours of **kumara**.

If you like chocolate biscuits, you'll adore **Tim Tams**. They're Australian in origin, but you're not visiting Aussie at this moment, so don't deny yourself the opportunity.

Hokey pokey ice cream. Apparently 'hokey pokey' for 'honeycomb' is Cornish in origin. And Cornwall's pretty good at ice cream, thinking about it. But again, if you're in NZ rather than Cornwall…

Milo. This may or may not effectively be Horlicks, as I've never tasted either. I happen to think it's a good name for a dog.

Chocolate fish. Not actually piscean in anything other than shape, these are a sort of pink nougat, covered in chocolate, and popular with big kids.

Anzac biscuits. Long associated with the Australian and New Zealand Army Corps, established in the First World War. There's a place for a full chapter on how these guys answered the call to fight alongside Britain in both world wars. Their gallantry, sacrifice, the debacle of Gallipoli, the Anzac Day services on April 25 each year...

But as this is a food chapter, just try the biscuits.

Marmite. Marmite "is a nutritious savoury spread that contains B vitamins, enjoyable in a sandwich, on toast, bread or even as a cooking ingredient."

In Britain, it's marketed, rather cleverly, on the basis that you'll either love it or hate it. I'm quite partial to it, but would still describe it as a salty, black, thick gloopy stuff, made from the yeast left over from the brewing process.

British Marmite is not to be confused with:

NZ Marmite. Which has a different flavour and not long ago, was in crisis. The factory that made it was damaged in the terrible 2011 Christchurch earthquake, late condemned, and thus was created the 2012 Marmite Shortage.

British and NZ Marmite are not to be confused with:

Vegemite. Which is Australian salty, gloopy yeasty stuff and quite disgusting.

Pavlova. Australia and New Zealand fights over who first thought to pair meringue, fruit and cream together. The rest of us can take whoever's side we like best and just enjoy.

It's possibly not very polite, by the way, to point out that 'kiwi fruit' had a previous life as Chinese gooseberries. It's rude to talk with your mouth full, anyway.

The flat white. It was either the Italians or the Americans gave the UK choice when it came to high street coffee (I'm not sure, but I suspect the former introduced to the latter and they brought it back across the Atlantic. This isn't a guide to Italy or the USA, so look it up yourself, if you want to know).

But coffee is sort of an art form Down Under and some of the best 'baristas' in the UK are Aussies or Kiwis. Possibly doing their 'OE' ('overseas experience,' as they call what we refer to, if we bother, as a 'gap year').

'Barista' is certainly Italian.

Anyway, the flat white is antipodean for 'like a latte only it actually tastes of coffee and there's no froth or chocolate

BREAKFAST: A WATERSIDE CAFÉ IN QUEENSTOWN –

sprinkles or other muck on top'. Many coffee chains and restaurants in the UK have caught on. Others are willing to be educated, if you ask nicely.

Fish and chips. Aka 'fush and chups'. Ok, the UK sees it as our national dish, but so does NZ. And if you're in the right place (Mangonui, for instance, boasts a 'world famous' fish restaurant) the fish will be whatever they caught a few hours earlier.

Freshly caught fish tastes about a zillion times better than something that's been in a freezer for months, so if you get the chance, try it.

Manuka honey. Manuka honey is produced in New Zealand by bees that pollinate leptospermum/ aka manuka/ aka tea tree bushes. Manuka honey has antibacterial power, thanks largely to something called methylglyoxal, and the strength of that is given a numbered rating: anything above 10 UMF (Unique Manuka Factor) is considered to be therapeutic.

Various studies have shown it is effective used on wounds – but that's medical grade, not straight out of the kitchen cupboard. It's a great ingredient in hand creams and similar lotions and supposedly good for a dry scalp, though I imagine applying honey to your hair is somewhat messy.

Personally, I like it for a sore throat. It's lovely full stop, but too expensive for most people to spread on their toast every morning.

World-famous in New Zealand

Not just the fish and chip shop: it's the slogan of L&P.

Otherwise **Lemon and Paeroa**.

It started with a natural spring in Paeroa. And now it's a lemonade-like drink, only much nicer, in a distinctive brown bottle with a yellow label.

Should you pass through Paeroa, there's a giant statue of the 'world-famous' bottle alongside the main road, (State Highway 2).

The town website claims it has "become one of the most well-known and photographed structures in New Zealand."

Town websites like to claim such things, but it's probably true. Though when a bus I was on stopped to let people take photos, I think I was the only passenger who'd actually heard of L&P. I happened to have a small bottle with me, half drunk, which I placed by the big one for contrast (*look closely to spot it!*). An idea which seemed to go down well with all who followed with their cameras.

Yeah, right

I'm not a beer drinker. I'm no expert on Speight's or Monteith's or Steinlager or Tui.

Sorry about that.

All I know is that Tui have the best adverts. A series of billboards with the punchline 'yeah, right'. E.g. 'Lotto – it wouldn't change me. Yeah, right'. 'Summer is more than beer, BBQs and bikinis. Yeah right'.

Wine. One of the UK cable channels was showing an episode of a 1970s sitcom, where the middle-class couple were having a party and dismayed when a guest brought a bottle of Australian wine.

I guess their idea of a classy wine would have been Liebfraumilch or Matteus rosé.

Nowadays, of course, wine from Australia and New Zealand is premium stuff in UK supermarkets, and rightly so.

New Zealand's wines are excellent. My favourites are sauvignon blanc (white) and pinot noir (red). If you've not already tried them, pick any from Sainsbury's to try as you read this book. If they don't make you want to visit for yourself…

Vineyards are a popular visitor attraction, by the way (can't think why!). For instance, Fullers not only run ferries from Auckland to Waiheke Island, they run a 'hop-on, hop-off' bus around its vineyards, along with guided tours, should you be worried it might be 'hop-on-roll-off' after a few tastings.

ONE OF THE VINEYARDS ON WAIHEKE ISLAND, A SHORT FERRY RIDE FROM AUCKLAND

HOBBITON – ON A SHEEP FARM IN MATAMATA

'The Wrong Island'

If you are short on time

Some years ago, before I'd ventured south of the Equator, a friend at work told everyone he was going to New Zealand for Christmas and the New Year. His girlfriend had relations near Auckland, and that's where they'd be staying.

He was really excited about this trip, and most other people in the office said nice things about it being a lovely idea. Bar one bloke whose response was: "You're going to the wrong island."

This wet blanket, who'd never crossed the Equator either, had it in mind that all the really good scenery was on the South Island – you know, all the Lord of the Rings bits.

It's true the South Island has lots and lots of totally awesome, spectacular scenery.

It's also true there's a scene in one of the LOTR films where someone falls off a cliff on the South Island and lands in a river just outside Wellington. That's movies for you. But just to make it clear: there is no 'wrong island'. Any more than if you were talking of visiting say Sussex, you'd be going to the 'wrong part' of the UK.

And while we're on the subject of Lord of the Rings: the photo at the start of Chapter Three and the one above were taken in Hobbiton – a sheep farm in Matamata, in the Waikato region of the North Island. There are various tours available in Wellington, including visiting the Weta Studios.

Plus of course, there are assorted tours from Christchurch and Queenstown. If there isn't already, there should probably be a book about all the LOTR locations and ways to explore them. I'm just saying if you only have time to visit a few places in New Zealand, then of course you are missing out, just as any visitor to the UK would be if all they had time to see was London. But equally, it doesn't mean you are visiting 'the less-worthwhile' location.

MY FAVOURITE SPOT IN WELLINGTON

Absolutely, positively Wellington

A seriously cool capital

No, no one knows what it means. It's a sort of advertising slogan thingy, dreamed up by someone to sell the place to tourists.

(You will also see 'Go Wellington' on the sides of buses. This is not an exhortation to cheer on the team: it's the name of a bus operator).

The sad thing is that Wellington does need selling.

To me, it is a fabulous place and probably my favourite city full stop.

But for most tourists, it's a one- or two-night stop, as they try to "do" NZ in a few weeks. Either somewhere to sleep before or after catching the ferry to/from the South Island. Or one to tick off the "I have visited" list, after a couple of hours in the Te Papa museum.

If that's all they see, they miss the cable car, the botanical gardens, parliament, two war memorials, the zoo, the wildlife sanctuary, a couple of other museums, an art gallery, the bucket fountain, lots of great walks, lots of great shops, Soames Island, the arts scene, the sports scene, assorted Lord of the Rings-related tours, and the pleasure of just sitting by the harbour with a flat white and a good book.

But they do get to see a neat museum. And the World's Biggest Squid.

So, you are a mighty denizen of the oceans deep. Fish fear you. You prowl the dark waters, a proud predator...

And end up in a display case in a museum in Wellington. A mass of putrid-looking red and white stuff with tentacles.

The legend on one end of the tank says: "Its skin is peeling, one eye is missing and it has shrunk a little."

And it is surrounded by gawpers, many of them muttering in disappointment: 'It's not as big as I thought it would be."

Poor squid.

He is in company with lots of stuffed things, now extinct; lots of Maori artefacts; a car made of corrugated iron; assorted works of art (some of it totally pretentious crap); a dead cow once used (while dead) to promote NZ milk in Britain; the skeleton of a racehorse; lots of info on earthquakes and the cheerful reminder that "nowhere in New Zealand is safe from natural disasters": and a sheepcam (giving you a sheep's-eye view of eating grass and being rounded up by a collie).

It's free to go round (there are visiting exhibitions you have to pay to see) and an enjoyable way to spend a wet afternoon.

Of which, there are plenty.

Wellington is famous for being windy. Indeed, when the airport people wanted to erect a naff hillside sign in lookalike letters saying 'Wellywood' (a nickname from the film industry success brought by Peter Jackson) and the citizens roundly objected, the public vote instead was in favour of a sign saying 'Wellington' with the final letters looking like they were taking off in the wind.

Which a lot of people suspected they would do for real.

However, the wind can come from different directions.

It is perfectly possible to go for a half-hour walk that starts with you getting drenched by sideways rain, but ends with you completely dry, the wind having changed direction and acting, in effect, like one of those automatic wash basins in public toilets, which spray water first, then turn on a hot air blower.

I wrote, during my first visit:

I like that:

- That in five minutes or so, walking, I can be sitting on the waterfront, watching the waves – or doing some Serious Shopping.

TAKE THE FIVE-MINUTE RIDE IN THE CABLE CAR UP FROM LAMBTON QUAY, IN THE CITY CENTRE, UP TO KELBURN, FOR FINE VIEWS. STROLL BACK DOWN THROUGH THE BOTANIC GARDENS

- That there's a department store with a piano in the women's clothing department, and a woman sitting there playing Tchaikovsky, while shoppers browse through blouses and peruse the shoes (sadly, now retired).

- That we walked up busy roads and walked back down a path through bush and woodland.

- That there are birds that sound like woodpeckers, and birds that make other strange calls, even though all you see are sparrows and seagulls.

- That there's a road crossing with a 'chalk outline' of a body in the middle: don't know if it's a council warning, or very funny graffiti.

- That they have Belisha beacons with circles of orange board on top instead of flashing lamps.

- That there are quirky statues and cool new buildings and neat conversions and no two houses are the same and nothing is what it used to be (this library used to be this, that museum used to be something else, those flats used to be whatever....)

- That people trying to sign me up for charities smile and say "sweet as" when I say politely I won't be giving them $5 a month, instead of continuing the guilt trip and hard sell .

- That all the clubs and bars are concentrated on one street, but don't seem to be filled with people saying: "What you looking at?" and trying to stick broken glasses in each other's faces.

- That it all feels laid-back.

- That it's raining sideways one minute and bright sunshine the next, rather than black clouds in the morning meaning it's going to p down all day.

- It's absolutely, positively Wellington (whatever that means) and I really like it.

KAPITI ISLAND, FROM WAIKANAE, ONE FINE CHRISTMAS DAY

Little baches, little baches

Of Kapiti and nature reserves

Wellington railway station is big and grand outside, but compact inside: eight or nine platforms all parallel. The early stages of the journey to the Kapiti coast are like any railway, really: backs of industrial units, weeds, and graffiti. But once you clear Wellington, it opens out into countryside. With sheep. NZ has long been famous for its lamb and its wool. But a lot of farmers have found there is more money in dairy.

And the money is in exporting produce. So you'll see lots of cows, and then find cheese is way dearer in the supermarkets than it is in the UK.

The hills reminded me of various parts of GB. The long, straight bit of coast didn't, because all you could see was sea, clouds, and rain, and I knew it was a lot more than 22-30 miles to the next-door neighbours.

The Kapiti coast is a popular place to retire to. It gets or shares its name with Kapiti Island. Which is a good time to talk about nature reserves.

The short version is that when NZ split off by itself a very long time ago, it took only birds and insects and fish and lizards and frogs with it.

With no mammals to eat them, a lot of the birds decided it wasn't worth the effort of flying or building nests in trees, so they forgot how to.

Then along came Man: first the tribes from the Pacific Islands, and a lot later from Europe. And they brought with them dogs and (accidentally) rats and later rabbits, and stoats and ferrets and cats and what with some of the men deciding the native birds tasted a bit like chicken, and the mammals liking an easy meal, the birds had a rough time of it.

BIRDS LIKE SADDLEBACK WERE WIPED OFF THE MAINLAND BUT SURVIVED ON ISLANDS. THIS ONE WAS ON ULVA ISLAND, OFF STEWART ISLAND

So now NZ has places like Kapiti as ideal nature reserves: if you poison all the mammals, they're gone and it's safe for the lizards and the ground-nesting, non-flying birds.

The poison used, 1080 (sodium fluoroacetate) isn't popular with everyone, but it seems the best solution anyone can come up with.

Meanwhile, it you go to Australia, you may look at the possums and think: "how cute".

If you see a possum in New Zealand, you are expected, if driving, to steer straight at it and splatter the thing into the tarseal.

Introduced for their fur, possums are the Number One pest in NZ. Apart from anything else, they are blamed for spreading bovine TB. And unlike badgers, similarly accused in the UK, the possums have no business being there.

On my first stay in the Kapiti town of Waikanae, I enjoyed an NZ family Christmas, seeing Christmas Day in at a local church service, and a barbecue lunch in the garden. No reindeer or snow, but the pohutukawa trees were in glorious flower: 'New Zealand's Christmas tree' in all its splendour.

My second stay coincided with another public holiday, and a local fête. If you want to see a country for real, forget the 'authentic' singing/dancing/whatever laid on for tourists and go to an event that local people go to. The log-sawing contests I saw there probably don't feature on the tourist trail, but they were the 'real' NZ.'

And the little baches?

A bach is a holiday hut. I'd guess from the Welsh 'bach,' or 'small,' except that it's pronounced as 'batch' rather than the Welsh 'bark'.

NZ families could buy a small plot of land and stick up a glorified shed. In recent years, land prices have soared, but everyone still loves the idea of the bach: a back-to-basics experience redolent of the early settlers who built a westernised country out of corrugated iron and no. eight wire.

DOLPHINS BEATING MY FINGER ON THE CAMERA SHUTTER, AT KAIKOURA

A whale of a time?

Local wildlife

My first whale-watching experience Canada taught me a lot... about whale-watching experiences

On the coach down to the dock, there was great excitement and anticipation, as we could see a bunch of whales doing their thing on the St Lawrence River.

By the time we'd all got on the boat, the whales had all pushed off somewhere else

It was a rainy day and after a while, fog closed in so thick you could barely see the other side of the boat, let alone anything else.

Meantime, one could observe human behaviour. If anyone saw something, everyone else would instantly rush to that side of the boat to see as well. Only there were so many people, just a few lucky folk got to see more than the backs of other people.

Rule no. 1 If you want to be able to see whales, dolphins, whatever, choose a boat with a small number of passengers.

At one point, a small, black, inflatable craft popped out of the fog as I was peering over one side of 'our' boat, startling me into a loud: "Oh!"

At which a bunch of people rushed over, thinking I'd seen a whale, then laughed because they thought I'd thought it was a whale.

Anyway. You can do whale-watching in NZ in Kaikoura. Where the boats aren't horribly over-crowded and I think they give you a refund if you don't see any whales. And you can go dolphin-watching in Paihia, where you need to be in the right spot to see anything beyond other passengers.

A lot of places also offer the chance to swim with dolphins or seals. Which I think is pretty intrusive on the part of humans, but does apparently prompt humour at iSITE tourist info centres when they get asked: "Do I have to be able to swim to go swimming with the dolphins?"

If you want to see dolphins, my best experience was in a small river-mouth town called Ballina, in New South Wales, Australia. Where I also got to see (wild) pelicans, ospreys, an assortment of river, sea and inland birds, and small blue crabs. Two popped up their heads in the river a few feet from me. And there were loads playing where the river met the sea. Totally free of boats or swimmers.

As this is supposed to be extolling NZ, I'd say to see dolphins, try a boat trip on the Doubtful Sound, or Kaikoura. Where you can also go for a walk, turn a bend, and find yourself a few feet from a basking sealion.

Just don't try pestering one of those to join you in a paddle.

'HAVE YOU GOT MY BEST SIDE?'

A PUKEKO IN ROTORUA

Trust me, that's not a tail

Native birds

So, you've paddled down from your Pacific island to this new place and it's full of big, fat, flightless birds with no fear of you as it hitherto had no predators. And what do you do?

Eat them, of course.

So, you're an 18th or 19th Century Brit, and you discover all these amazing, unique, fabulous birds, and what do you do?

Trap them, stuff them, put them in museums, and turn them (feathers) into hats

And with a forest teeming with tui and bellbirds and saddlebacks and kereu and filled with wonderful birdsong, what else do you?

Think: "What this place REALLY needs is a few sparrows."

And blackbirds, and pigeons, and swallows, and mynah birds. All of which you are far more likely to see than the bird everyone associates with New Zealand, the kiwi.

There are nature reserves that do nocturnal guided tours looking for kiwi, but they tend to be fully booked before you even find they exist.

The simplest way to see one is to go to a visitor attraction that has a kiwi house. If you stand very quietly, letting your eyes adjust to the dark, you should be rewarded by seeing one or more of these crazy-looking birds rooting around in its enclosure.

If you charge in, as a lot of visitors do, talking excitedly and saying: "It's really dark in here, I can't see anything. Can you see anything?" you probably won't, and will give up after 30 seconds and leave, disappointed.

Yes, kiwi houses are great place to observe people as well as birds.

My favourite overheard comments in kiwi houses:

"I can see a rabbit."

"I can see its tail."

There are several species of kiwi, by the way, not counting the red plastic one I had as a child that was an advertising item for shoe polish.

One bird that isn't shy is the Australasian gannet. Cape Kidnappers, in the Hawkes Bay region on the North Island, is home to the largest and most accessible gannet colony in the world. There are guided tours, including rides along the beach to get there on a tractor trailer. If you decide to simply walk, check the tide times. Seriously, it's a long walk there and back (allow six hours) and can only be done at low tide as you don't want to get cut off.

The gannets, by the way, have a six-foot wingspan and while you can't, for obvious reasons, get too close to their main nesting areas, the smell is pretty distinctive even from a distance.

Pretty much my favourite bird is the pukeko. It's big, it's blue (with a red beak and forehead), and it plods about in swamps and public parks. It won Forest and Bird's Bird of the Year competition in 2011. You'll know one when you see one.

You already know what a penguin looks like, right? Well, New Zealand has three species of them: next stop south is the Antarctic, after all. If you visit the city of Dunedin, look out for wildlife tours that can give you an incredible close up view of the penguins, along with sea lions and fur seals in their natural habitat. While you're in the area, visit the Royal Albatross Centre. Dunedin's Taiaroa Head is the only mainland Royal Albatross breeding colony in the world and if you thought the gannets were big, their wingspan can be more than three metres.

FOUND ONLY IN NEW ZEALAND, YELLOW-EYED PENGUINS ARE THE WORLD'S RAREST

'Glowworm' sounds prettier

An underground adventure

If you take pleasure in being terrified, there are plenty of ways you can get your kicks in New Zealand, such as white-water rafting and base jumping off Auckland's Sky Tower. Why anyone would want to fall 192 metres straight down on a wire, I've no idea. But if depths are more your thing than heights, I can recommend the Waitomo caves. This underground labyrinth has stalactites and stalagmites, streams, waterfalls – and twinkling constellations of glowworms.

Except they're not really glowworms. They are a gnat larvae (arachnocampa luminosa) unique to New Zealand. They produce sticky lines, like a spider's thread (hence the 'arachno') to catch insects, which are attracted by the bioluminescent glow.

There are ways to see them that don't involve pulling on a wetsuit and dragging a huge inflatable ring around an underground stream for three hours, but black-water rafting is a very satisfying adventure.

EXPLORING WAITOMO CAVES, COURTESY OF THE LEGENDARY BLACK WATER RAFTING CO

THE SKY TOWER CAFÉ IS 182 METRES UP, WITH PEOPLE BOING-ING PAST THE WINDOWS

WAIPOUA FOREST: I'VE ANONYMISED THE WOMAN HUGGING THE TREE, FOR HER PRIVACY

Hebe heaven

Flora great and small

Hebe, parahebe, phormium, various pittosporum, coprosma, fuchsia excorticata, hoheria, corokia, manuka (leptospermum), libertia, lancewood, olearia, pseudopanax lessonii, pseudowintera colorata, podocarpus, astelia and haloragis erecta (toatoa). And that's just my back garden.

I even have a small pohutukawa in a pot in my bedroom, as I fear it wouldn't survive year-round outdoors. I wrap the manuka and libertia in fleece in winter.

What I haven't got is arthropodium (rock lily) or clianthus maximus (kaka beak), because the slugs ate them. While myosotidium hortensia (Chatham Island forget-me-not), kept out of the way of slugs, hates being wet and rotted over the winter.

Meanwhile, look into back gardens in New Zealand (where it is legal and non-intrusive to do so!) and you'll likely see hydrangeas, cineraria, geraniums... Because gardeners the world over like something different from native species.

For that reason, you will also see over there, in full flower in summer, agapanthus and montbretia (crocosmia) growing like weeds in all sorts of places they aren't really wanted. Just as buddleia davidii is very pretty and attracts bees, but is regarded as an invasive species in the UK, sprouting from cracks in pavements and walls of derelict buildings.

I have a book on 100 Best Native (NZ) Plants, running to 376 pages, and 150-page book on hebes – I say that to illustrate why I'm not going to go into great detail on the subject.

If you like botanic gardens, I can recommend the ones in Wellington and Dunedin, which are close to the city centres. Get the cable car in Wellington to the top for great views, then stroll down through the botanic garden, and treat yourself to coffee and cake in or outside the café at the bottom.

If you like trees, well, there are plenty of forests, but a 'must-see' is Waipoua Forest, the largest kauri forest in New Zealand and home to Tane Mahuta, the

DUNEDIN BOTANIC GARDENS, ON A CLOUDY DAY

"Lord of the Forest". It is 51.5 metres tall, four metres in diameter, and has a girth of 13.77 metres. Te Matua Ngahere, "Father of the Forest," was a sapling around 3,000 years ago and has a girth of 16.4m.

I've blocked the face of the woman in the photo, as she was a stranger and may not appreciate being in this book.

If you want to own a souvenir that is 45,000 years old but looks and feels great, buy something made of swamp kauri: kauri trees preserved perfectly in peat swamps. When polished it is a gorgeous golden colour, with a beautiful grain, and is so tactile you want to stroke it! The Ancient Kauri Kingdom showroom and retail outlet at Awanui has a staircase carved from a 50 tonne section of one swamp log. Me, I just have a small, heart-shaped box.

HEBE, ON STEWART ISLAND

CHRISTCHURCH HAD LOTS OF HERITAGE BUILDINGS. MOST OF THE CBD HAD TO BE DEMOLISHED AFTER THE DREADFUL 2011 EARTHQUAKE

The Shaky Isles

Don't panic, but..!

I was woken about ten to nine by a loud bang and a sharp jolt. Followed by a shaking that felt like the spin cycle of a washing machine. I was thinking: "Why is the wall moving? Oh, it must be an earth.." At which it stopped.
My first earthquake!!! 5.1 on the Richter scale and about 50km down.
Actually, in five visits, it's the only earthquake that I've felt. It's not the only I've experienced and anyone heading to New Zealand needs to be aware that while you may be as likely to get caught by one as you are to win the lottery*, New Zealand is rocked by tremors all the time. Most of them too weak to notice.
To put some figures on that: I have an app that records NZ earthquakes and as I type this, on a typical day, it shows there were nine in the past 24 hours, one of which, at 3.3, 20km down, near Gisborne, led to 96 reports by people to the app company – as did one of 4.7, 12km deep, off the coast 60km north of Milford Sound. Others weren't reported at all.
I repeat, this is a random day. Another random day shows 12 quakes, from 2.4 to 4.2, from Wairoa on the east of the North Island to Milford Sound again, near the 'bottom left' of the South Island.
If that worries you, there's been nothing in the 'strong' category since April, while the 7.8 November 2016 Kaikoura quake that caused so much damage was 'extreme' (with nine of the aftershocks in the following few hours 'severe').
A 4.6 magnitude 'strong' earthquake at Kaikoura in May was felt as far away as Nelson, with someone there reporting the "whole building shook."
Two people died in the November 2016 Kaikoura quake, which saw the town cut off because of landslides, and the seabed rise in places. There was structural damage in Wellington, too, with the Insurance Council of

New Zealand reporting in February 2017 that private insurers had to that date received business claims valued at more than $900 million (65 per cent from Wellington). That's business claims, to that date.

Far worse, in recent history, was the February 22, 2011 Christchurch earthquake, which killed 185 people (most of them in one building) and injured thousands. It came five months after a 7.1 quake that had damaged buildings but spared people, probably because most were in bed and not out in the street.

More than half of the buildings in the central business district have since been demolished, with the damage bill from the two quakes put at roughly $40 billion NZD.

I was in Wellington when the second one struck, shopping: didn't feel a thing and first I knew was hearing a shop assistant on a phone saying: "The cathedral's gone this time."

On the plane home, I met a couple who'd been in Christchurch that afternoon, and had planned to go up the cathedral tower. They debated: "Cathedral or gift shop first?" Chose the latter. And thus were safe in a shop when the quake struck, minutes later.

*(not exact odds: I've no idea of the exact odds, depends partly on whether you even do the lottery)

Sound advice

If you want to know what to do in an earthquake, there's some advice at: www.getthru.govt.nz/disasters/earthquake/ (other disasters are available on the website)

Red sky at night

The clear message given by the awesome displays in Wellington's Te Papa museum is that there is nowhere in New Zealand where you are truly safe from natural disasters. The fascinating displays cover, not only earthquakes, but also volcanoes.

Of which NZ has lots. Some of them still active. Ruapehu, where the North Island ski fields are, has had about 60 minor eruptions in as many years, with some major ones in 1995 and 1996 and a hydrothermal eruption and lahars (mudflows) in 2007.

Volcanoes are monitored constantly, and there's an alert system to get people out of the way if things look to be heating up.

One 'unlikely' volcano they are monitoring is Lake Taupo. Taupo is a 'supervolcano', and when it 'went up' a couple of thousand years ago, the Romans and Chinese recorded unusual red sunsets that may have been caused by it, which all NZ got a coating of ash. The lake is acutally a caldera (collapse crater), with magma chamber between 6 and 8 km below. It looks, well, like a lake. Apart from the fact that around the shore, you'll see bubbling, boiling mud pools, fenced off with helpful warning notices that you really, really, really, don't want to put your hand or anything you hold dear anywhere near them.

DON'T PADDLE HERE!

You'll be glad to know the experts say the chance of Roman-times-scale eruption are "very, very low"

A silver lining today

One terrible earthquake led, by chance, to a modern-day 'gem'. In February 1931, the Hawkes Bay/Napier earthquake killed 261 people, injured thousands, and devastated the region.

It meant everything had to be rebuilt, resulting in Napier today being able to call itself the Art Deco Capital. There are festivals and walks and tours. Or, you can just wander around with a camera and be totally spoiled for choice: there are 147 Art Deco Buildings to snap.

A GEYSER LETS OFF STEAM AT TE PUIA MAORI CULTURAL CENTRE AND GEOTHERMAL PRESERVE, ROTORUA

Hubble, bubble...

Rotorua, a geothermal wonderland

One of my favourite places in NZ is Rotorua. To the point now where, if ever I smell sulphur (say, strong drain-cleaner), it triggers instant memories of that amazing town.

The smell comes from the geothermal activity that makes the place so amazing and causes steam to rise from manhole covers, people's back lawns, and is responsible for bubbling, boiling mud pools and geysers that shoot high into the air. Oh, and some awesome lakes in stunning colours (thanks to geology). And hot pools and health spas you can relax in. And there's a big lake, and a museum, and a park with croquet and a wildlife park, and things for adrenalin junkies… newzealand.com lists 39 tours and 78 activities, and they're not 'scraping the barrel' to come up with that many.

There are also Māori 'cultural experiences' such as singing and the haka (war dances). Not my bag anywhere, to be honest. Contemporary/traditional Māori arts and crafts, yes, 'cultural performances,' no, but then I've never been into dancing or watching other people do so. I remember hearing an anecdote on a radio programme where the 'traditional song' tourists were treated to somewhere in the world actually translated as something like: "Give us all your money and go away"! I'm not saying that applies anywhere in Rotorua, but I did once get chatting to a British tourist who said he and his wife had gone for the whole 'haka and ground-cooked food' thing, only to see one of the dancers eating a McDonald's burger round the back afterwards.

THE PANCAKE ROCKS OF PUNAKAIKI, ON THE WEST COAST OF THE SOUTH ISLAND

Top to toe

The Ends. And the middle

I've lived in the UK almost all my life and there are lots of places I've never visited. So, if you are thinking of 'doing' New Zealand in two-three weeks, either focus on one smallish area, or accept you'll spend a lot of time driving while only getting a taster of the country. Five visits, 17 weeks in total, 'circumnavigating' both islands along the way, and I've only scraped the surface.

It's also all I've done in this book. I could write a chapter each on Auckland, Bay of Islands, Coromandel, Tauranga, Taupo, New Plymouth, Napier… Christchurch, Dunedin, Queenstown, Te Anau, the Sounds… and lots more. But then it would be a very long book, and not just 'a taster'.

If you stay at the top end of the North Island, Cape Reinga is the furthest you can get (the most-northerly tip is a scientific reserve) and the place where two oceans meet. Māori tradition has it that this is where their spirits return to the ancestral homeland and there is something special about seeing a swirling clash of water and realising it's the Pacific and the Tasman colliding.

If you get to the bottom end of the South Island, Stewart Island (or Rakiura) is a peaceful spot to get away from it all. It's 30km south of the South Island, you can get to it by ferry or light aircraft (15-20-minute flight over far too fast), and it has a population of around 400. The list of activities is pretty much limited to variations of 'walk,' and 'look at birds' – and it is excellent for both. Lot of people do it as a day trip: waking up to fabulous dawn chorus, and tramping around with a camera, it's a great place to chill for a few days.

Wherever you go, have a great time. And should you wish to take along a personal tour guide…

THE VAST AND UNSPOILT WILDERNESS OF DOUBTFUL SOUND, FIORDLAND

And finally...

Acknowledgements

All my trips to New Zealand were funded by spending a large chunk of an inheritance. And made possible by an employer who allowed me to take a three-month sabbatical the first time, and to take three-and-bit weeks of my annual holiday entitlement in one block in each of the following four Februaries.

I am grateful to both. And a big thank you to anyone reading this book, too. I hope you enjoy it.

©Cassie Graham, 2017. All rights reserved.

Printed in Poland
by Amazon Fulfillment
Poland Sp. z o.o., Wrocław